Emporium

Aditi Machado

Emporium
Aditi Machado

Nightboat Books/New York

ISBN: 978-1-64362-029-9

Design and typesetting by Tiffany Malakooti
Text set in Portrait, Baskerville, and Caxton

Cataloging-in-publication data is available from
the Library of Congress

Nightboat Books
New York
www.nightboat.org

"Herewith the prologue:"

I came along a silk route. I came low like low things. Slow, farcical
leaves rimmed the trees. Some chic birds. I came along a long way,
bolstered by merchants and prophylactics and an obscure shade
that became my practice.

Sometimes I'd stop
to confer with magnolias and find the writing on the margin
creeping in. Or I'd look up at the archive wandering hysterically
like a womb. I'd stop at markets where rank matadors offered me
coins.

Magnalia! Magnalia! I heard those bards, I loved
those shops, little bourgeois vessels of amnesia and maybe
lockets. And sometimes

I'd stop at theatres
and watch the facsimile faces twatting by, the customary graffito
on a restaurant tile. I'd forget my resistances, small wrists, and gussy
up my deadlocked tongue. Nothing to see here, I'd say, but
virtuoso shrubs.

Along the silk route upon which I came came
the very neat devices of a memoirist or politico. The silkiness
of the route was of an old time, colored like old, color
photographs, with seepages into the corners of sight.

Silk either
wore me down or bore me out of a series of vacancies in which
I scanned beaches. I was 'caught.' Who 'caught' me
but a phantom certainty, 'certainty like a quality of gems
and cautious doctrines'? This was my distraction and
having to tighten my belt and all that. And yet

I was arriving,
words appearing on points of fact. Prickly or vine-like, I proposed
this and that. I was told nation or rhapsody or wear simple clothes.
I heard those statements as limpid fugues, traumas wandering
out of musical bars. I had no purchase on those points.

For a while
it was impossible to wear silk. I'd look up at the ruched sky,
I'd consider the Jesuitic races, the long lines of vox sniff-sniffing,
the climate refusing to change, the clematis reminding me
I was to pursue a sound. I was to steal

　　　　　　　　　　　　　　　　　along, I was to barter
my socialisms for some mastic or gâteau slaked with rum or
a velvet speculum or any sort of very erudite and algebraic,
any sort of very telluric sort, a sort of, any sort, a sottise,
any sort of sottise. So

　　　　　　　　　　　　　　I bartered my socialisms for something
hierarchic, something hemorrhagic, hagio-cratic, her-metical, hell,
helical, her-heretical, hire, hire, hieroglyphic, had her, hatter, heter-
onomous, hire, hair, hairy. It was a hairy time.

　　　　　　　　　　　　　　　　　　　And my bush
was a mulberry bush. It occasioned silk. Silk was a duration. I
unpacked it. Finally arriving, tender glissade. Lowing in the fields,
rennet skies. Up ahead, the emporium, up ahead. All those
haptic divinities. All those sounds I came to quell,

　　　　　　　　　　　　　　　　　　　　asking,
questioning, comment, comment, comment, quel, quelle
laine, quel lin, quel coton, quel satin, quel crin, quel chanvre,
quel cachemire, quel velours, quel tweed, quelle flanelle,
quelle dentelle, quel calicot, quelle mousseline, quel
serge, quelle jute, quel jacquard, quel brocard,
quel cuir, quelle soie, quel soi, quelque soit,
quelque soie, quelle soi

"collusion
cusp this"

Social Gesture

First I agree to look upon the city.
There is a rhythm properly incensed.
A church rings clear through my doubts.
I decline all things in respect to how I see them.
The dative reigns. I like that pileup
like ornaments of queens. Then I look again
at the heap, then I struggle to see
how each body is separate, no precision
that isn't imprecision.

First I agree to touch that treeline, measure that
awesomely obtuse leafiness, the way psalms
build height into it. First it measures me

across a distance. A treeline internal
to somnolence beyond which could not grow
any more obtuse my reason for being.

Then there's a shift in the treeline.

Then I look again upon the city. Somebody's body
is unlucky in that precise manner by which is meant
plainness. Somebody else's thinking is in gutters
or nervous systems. What's the matter, I ask,
as in what's a matter.

A þing, a throng.

So she has a þing with her and thus a body.
And they have a þing with them and thus a body.
A volume of sound accompanies the rites.

Amid the failing narrative I go to the movies
and can't say where in the mob I'm not,
the film so draws an endlessness.

Outside the poet cries, spell me!
Spell me out, weather, I got
the whiplash you got!

First a word, then an idea. First a body,
then an idea, then a word. First touching,
then more touching. Touching as the precision
of bodies delving into imprecision, 'this strange
affinity.'

First an organ senses. First 'sensation
not sense.' First singing

as affinity for trees or skylines
scales a territory. First a refrain
grounds as an ossuary grounds,

then she leaps, 'first then.'

First 'the sea indents the universe,' then my body is
a beach from which I look into foam, an inquiry proceeds
a simile along its likeness.

Then my bodies are ideas. Finger them.

Then I hedge, I stalk a highway.
Its terror turns the landscape round.

A new history, I think, a new territory,
I'll plant a flag that dies perennially.

And so on it's gone, thronged. In medias res
as in that apparition of faces. These are flourishes.

And outside the poet cries,
    look at juniper
    and make gin,
    that's my skill.

    The city enjambs
    the forest, how
    triste, how truant.

"found in the archive wandering hysterically:

"this old thing"

Emporium

As if I could simply pass through
the carts, hand myself over to some notions
piled on a cart, trade away certain desires
amid the silk & squid, certainty
like a quality of gems & cautious doctrines,
trade away myself—wouldn't be
too unlovely, in derivative light, lamps all
succulence above the general meat, would it,
butchers?—for tartan weather or any gridlike
complexity of time & back to square
home,

       the sugar makes a mound there
as once bright pyramids & the smells here
are superlative, all brine & depth as though
one upon the other we effloresced. &
the tapestries descend & wouldn't we
endlessly such velvet landscapes buy?

As if I could simply
stay here with
the provocations.

& if I did
what would I
sell?

& would I look at the mongers & hooks,
would I love these men, I would.

Love now is not so corralled & distance dreams
itself out of longevity.

Bowie strings a violin.
A neat bird suggests the littoral.
The limes settle into excellence.

Come on, eros arrowly. Why not
the emporium?

(The chief comparison is to a quality of light. The people have not poured in as light, won't pour out. The poets stall. Vending short texts & long texts, scarves run through bodily fluids. We live in the clusterfuck. The chief definitions are here now. The chief epics are of markets spinning, carnival eyes. Pastimes replete with blinds. The chief binaries fold & unfold. The garden in the kitchen is in the street. Sweet herbs & cow patties. Sweetness the provocation & chief style of the poets. *The extent to which history inscribes industrial products is perfume,* one writes, cupping silver. *Petals, petroleum, idioms profuse & tangled in the neck, a goblet. History paves the emporium & porous the gemlight.*)

& says the purveyor, best not study such shapes
but silk, to me of silks, of the brushing of blouses
against silken nipples, of between her legs the stolen
red, & even money isn't quite like money when silk
buys me or have I, it, or has it
blended in the fabrics of, when there was a room
for me to try on the, there was weather then
& now too, it's silking my mind, & the 'qualities
as they continue are the silk under the hand,' reads
the libel, silk, that's the dual error & shock
of new precision, an involuntary, not involuntary
exactly, but desired, frisson, I've pulled the brocade
off the rack.

Accents ascend the soundfield, bonny
suns climb the vaulted ceiling; magnets.

My senses, cursive, seek an angle;
sensing danger, name an enemy nylon.

Or did I mean history? Did I mean shale?
& of what is it collaged? How does it cohere?
Sudden queries, sudden as vendors, do they sell
fruit, sell textile? I've been so exact
I've cut corners. O obsolescence, o light brain
sifting the accidental tree, I desire cinema
in a sense all factories sense
the dilemma. Ought I
shove off?

The emporium moves by shift of wind.
Shuffles its constituents. Atomizes
in concept, not material, yet how suggestive,
how like a pleasant sea, that fine spray.

"I was told

"nation"

Steady.

Steady now, a sense is pealing out the surface areas.

Observe here the fit expressions, as germane as botanic.

Here a faith in images still, and moving, you observe nothing quite proves prosody but people feel rhythm in their bodies.

The body is pronounced bawdy.

And here a faith in materials I too cagily profess.

And then 'the sense / faints.'

Fold this.

Steadily you discover exteriors. Fold them.

Continual and cheapened light of the electric kind suffuses most areas in which you remain.

In some sense you are reporting on a country.

What do you observe?

You observe observation, its obstacles.

Forms of envy.

Narrative growing out the landscape constrainedly.

A seasonal negation inducing absence.

A relation blooms in this landscape full of abuses.

The people aren't errant, they're erratic.

Terror takes them.

The air is filled with amazing becomings, Marquezian butterflies.

Fold this.

This is not a truth but a way, a movement—simply—moving futures into fuchsias.

"or"

"rhapsody"

Let us exercise our vocal cords.
Let us draw them out
limbs.

Let us say there is always a longer or shorter
tress, always congruities, blissful, bitter
rhythms, sprung onions splitting, violins in
harmony that is harmonic, chaos that is chaotic,
in sense that is sensible, in here it inheres, out there
rapid rabbits. Let us labor under these notions
as under the cantus planus factory whine.

Let us stumble around, humming, stumbling, humming.

Then something in the shape of leaves,
something in the touching of 'red.'

Is it subversive?

Let us hesitate with 'red.' Let us feel it out
with the feeling which we are. It is a panic
in the full field. This outward loping, is it
making it?

Is it filling it? Is it making it
explicit?

/ x x / || / x x /

A kind of horror at tubers.

A tipping against, as though I against
clement green, appears symmetrical
from way off in the distance I devise.
Do you know this desire? It's a bit like
leaning into something. Sometimes
experience is like that,
nutritional. The thing is, I'm developing
an accent. I don't like it.

I try to narrow it, I hesitate. I try to sing it,
I hesitate. Everyone is about to kneel,
pyrrhic. I mean, the congressional tune,
it seduces my agnostic body. So I'm a little
late to it, but I'm there. I get the bells
orchestrate law. I get the centaurs
are asters. Their conglomeration
awaits our easter gathering. Sunlight
comes through the heightened bulbous
assemblage. In a second I'll commune,
but there is in me a little antinomian
flecked desire. So I hesitate a second,
then go out with them. Into quite the
sunlight, spreading sort of around
very lackadaisical. Very like a floral
spigot. Someone opens the countryside
that opens the aural. Against
the church on the hill.

To which the faithful voluptuously
turn. Which, if they lose, to what
will they genuflect? A deck
built slowly of atheism in the moss-
induced decoalescing sonic
purpose someone decolonized?
It's like innocence way off
in the distance, distorted.
I don't believe in lapsing,
but it's like that.

Like I'm shifting out
of one desire
into another,
asynchronous.

And the things that carry me back
do not carry me back whole.
I try to rest in the depressions,
landscapes under duress, as by eros
eroded, the guttural roses spring
forms familiar and foreign, thorns
iambic, limbic the rows.
It does not flatten out.

And broken lies the golden vox spilling रस ਠੜ
filling it रस ਠੜ making it explicit. Rust rings it.

And says Donatvs, the stem is air stricken sensible
to ears, in so far as their power to hear is.
Wistfully I say each stem
is wrought from the clipping and the air is stricken
with it and is worked into a stem. The stem is
conspicuous or it is fuzzy. It is conspicuous
when with meaning it is clipped: I herald
those weapons, I herald that man. It is fuzzy
when without it is: cows lowing, horses
neighing, hounds hounding, trees
bristling, ET CETERA (Ælfric).

/ x x / ‖ / x x /

Let us make it lovely again. Let us make gardens and lakes
a variorum of some eternal para-
nomasiac, some perfect para-
dogmatic, perfect para-
dise.

Let us stumble around
this place that's humming,
humming. Counting
the stems and the
howling, hollering,
the refrains, o
the terrible refrains.

We're in a musical, thinking.

/ x x / ‖ / x x /

Rhapsody—or rhubarb?

Scant difference between some flowers
and the heads of cauliflowers the fingers get
herbaceous rubbing against. If I could get
ecstatic I would by the low soft
weeds, the hard oracular orifices of tree bark.
Some landscapes under duress
predict this atonal sky.

Scant difference between flowers.
The canned cool metal slightly
curves, of trash receptacles.
meadow interregna, strange
fanciful flights, toward toward.

Where the rhubarb field is not so bright
red as you would think, not so precise
or fulminating, too much green sticks
out, stems and leaves like a fuzz
of voices, watery incarnadine,

here where the sounds so simplify
the milieu into that wetness there,

here I stumble
to approximate the durations of others, to appear
of the same time as though of space,
I worry terribly, I hesitate, I lose my measure, a juice
trickles down my side,

रस ਠਂ੍ਤ

Like
I get I'm out of tune.

/ x x / || / x x /

Let us think.

In the speaking of it,
it eludes.

Is it—a lark?

It fills it. It makes it explicit. It does not flatten out.

Is it
just spin?

Like origins.

Tender regress. Celestial pablum.
I like this myth.

/ x x / ‖ / x x /

Something somethings.

Purified something
exerts pressure
on the sometimes vital
organs.

Some systems proffer
all vowels alliterate and in all
prose a prosody. I think proclivities
by which ordinary speech becomes
vibratory pollinate such systems.
I'm only looking for a little
homophony. Others, honey.

Ever since the accent I find my mouth
in places unforeseen. I'm given to
the understanding of others. It's not futile,
but it is strange in the dark to speak the dark rolling
the gilded rowels, the stars of blood catching on
the dank-ytressèd trees. Against my nature
stand all possible drones.

Origins: sovereigns:
oranges.

For in the beginning there was a sound and the sound
was good. I licked it. It made sense. I milked it.
But you see the war unsettled it. A clean historical
break right down the landing strip of it. I licked it.
Something in the shape of it, something in the
touching of it. The music went out of it. And my desire
for it, a widening gyre. Lyre? You sense it? We lost
our measure. I licked it. This myth.

"or wear simple clothes."

("Reader—a job
has taken us
up.

We are a

shrink!")

"Marceline?" says she, "that's mostly cotton." We have left her a pile of cloths in the corner mottled by the angular dusk visiting peripherally. For the moment, it is enough to say: she considers us a strange deacon, we minister ably. Location: she is centrally located. She does not mention muslin, she fears velvet, has had fourteen confinements . . . . . .

. . . .

. . . .

. . . . Today she worships the word GLOVE, esp. when marked w/ the use of a woman. We have not read in weeks & are most attentive to outward aspects, the mellow insinuation of light through the closures bursting open as by buxom strain from the ambrosial child within, for the effects of the child are upon everything now & the less we read the more tend the reverberations of our impecunious subject. Presently she deranges the furniture. A sudden, a pure stillness. . . . .

. . . .

. . . .

. . . . Now a dream. But whose? Red zone beyond the scrim. Absence of reading is a bit lacerating . . . .

. . . . "I feel my throat," today she says, "swelling. I feel my belly swelling, then I lose consciousness. When I crush it, there's a pang, then there's a climax, I am as tho drunk! I tremble but not from fear," she—mimicking a frisson—says, "I don't think about the wrong thing I just did. I just sit apart from everyone else so I can touch it. That's when I'm caught." Then she says, "When I finish I become sad. My limbs are all aching". . . . .

. . . . . . Her intellect is dull. Periods of disillusion appear to rouse her perversions. For the moment, it is enough to say: degeneration, depression, electrification by silk. . . . .

. . . .

. . . .

. . . .

. . . .

. . . . Mottled
by light. . . . .
. . . .
. . . .
. . . .
. . . .
. . . . Mottled by
shadow. . . . .
. . . .
. . . .
. . . . Pile of . . . .
. . . .
. . . .
. . . .
. . . . .Sudden, pure stillness—she's awake.
We haven't read in weeks & are attentive to outward aspects of the
abyssal room in which we mind the child & the child dissimulates. Bare
shelves. Embarrassing lack of speech. Kidskin gloves, preferred when
marked w/ the use of a woman. Adoration of the left glove. Desecration
of the right. Semaphores . . . .
. . . .
. . . .
. . . .
. . . . Sometimes . . . .
sometimes we wield her like a sieve against the light, afternoon mesh, &
are able to view a distant feature such as a water tower. This is our
human interest, which vibrates . . . .
. . . .
. . . .
. . . . Today we note brightnesses of the

eye, a pouting, certain kinds of locutions & retorts. "Calicot," she says, "cretonne, these don't make sounds, little cries of nothing." What did she dream? She dreamed thickly furred animals. We haven't read in weeks. The sensation is of violet leaking thru the blinds. Epidermal sensations are necessary and decisive . . . .
. . . .
. . . .
. . . .
. . . .
. . . .
. . . .
. . . .
. . . .
. . . .
. . . .
. . . . When she tears silk, it is not a sadistic violence but the violence of trying to understand it. . . . .
. . . . Mottled dusk. Angled confusion. Inverse inflorescence into which the pile of cloths is deranged. This is . . . .
. . . . intense . . . .
. . . .
. . . .
.Presently, she pees. It wets the dress. She palpates the textile. We offer to her the following anecdote: our comrade, ever since he became impotent, is given to dipping his penis in milk and this gives to him the sensation of velvet. No erection follows. He drinks the milk w/ indifference. The sensation of velvet, we tell her, is not the sensation of light. "Light?" she squawks. "I'm perverse? You're perverse!" . . . .
. . . .
. . . .
. . . . An expressive manner of speaking, an ingenious way of doing, & a flexibility w/ time, place, & person as only the practice of an ancient passion wd suggest. Enough to say: copacetic. Continual mottling of the cloth piles. Wet cerebrum. . . . .
. . . .
. . . .

. . . .
. . . .
. . . .
. . . .
. . . . .We are keen to read & therefore
distracted from the present. In wielding the silk, she has soiled it,
evidently by placing it against her genitalia. We refrain from asking
precisely what sort of satisfaction . . . .
. . . .
. . . .
. . . .
. . . .
. . . . It is
sufficiently clear the cloth does not intercede for the masculine body. In
fact, it appears to agitate of its own accord, by dint of its solidity,
brilliance, odor, & sound, properties nevertheless secondary to its
tactile qualities, which are bountifully responsive to the suggestions of
a refined epidermis. . . . . She
is organically motivated. She is sensorio-censorious . . . .
. . . .
. . . .
. In the absence of reading everything vibrates out of orbit. The
epidermis feels itself becoming passive. In the absence of reading milky
description coats us. This is intense. Picturing it in the mind—
mimicking a frisson—cannot compensate for it. Palpating the textile is
necessary here. Must the silk, we ask, be clean? Would a bit of mottled
silk be entirely, we ask, devoid of charm? Would a man clad in silk do,
as silk does? Singe of activity on the brow lit by angular light. "Light?"
she squawks. We know, we're perverse. But is she aroused by the
animals in her dreams? Does she associate fresh silk w/ some abstract
notion of virginity? . . . .
. . . .
. . . .
. . . .
. . Other e.g. of haptically stimulating materials: roses, milt.

Criminal Archive 17.3, pp. 132-136

A Receipt

spuds
raffia
iodine
rock crab
fiduciary
limes
pansies
quinine
flecked
gum
persimmons
fenny
rack of
lamb
deck of
mortuary
cards
rags to
stuff up
yr red time
12 annas

"Herewith the memory

"and its epitaph:"

QUOD
VULGO
GELATINAM
VOCAMUS

Experiment with Aspic

It commences. Here
   it is endless. Mostly
poverty. Parallel to
the railway track.
Manure, procession,
conniptions. It is crisp.
   A labyrinth. It is here
it commences. Lac,
it is said. Or albumen.
      Gourds, chikus, com-
prehensions of ripeness.
What's fresh, what's
   not, under the same
feckless auspices.
Luxury, it is said, moves,
      sometimes, at midday.
Mellow the light cast on
such euphemistic striations.
         On the goathooks
(up ahead), on the garlands
      (up ahead up ahead).
The muffled scene of death
to which the lines proceed,
curved. Citrus curling up
   the light, so tart it is.
   But here, here where it
commences, here, from where
the lines, endless, proceed,
      here the voices, here
the prices. Lacquer on this
produce, surreal photography,
tainted reverie. Nothing clean
yet, presence implied, not seen.
         It proceeds, an extreme
   intelligence can be held
in the hands, is. Slight burn

from the citrus, slight build
from up the ground. Euphemism
    for shanty. Euphemism for
        indigence. Skinny body,
slender bean, sturdy drumsticks
    snap. Nothing clean, yet
the causal knives luxuriate.
Lone jackfruit, abandoned
beehive. Nightshade in terror
    of being shook. The lymph is
anxious. The child rears her
        ugly head, slow capacity
for memory. Lacquer, she says.
    Lacquer on this. This kind of
traffick is difficult to curb. Her skin
is light, her mother's translucent.
    This is how it begins, the acts
of comprehending things, softening,
    into the basket, plastic,
            the voiceless hellos, a
        tendency, hushed.
An impossible sculptural
    aspect her eyes laminate.
Things mature along
    this aisle that's endless.
And she too, in the town
called Fraser, opposite
the police station and the
pork shop, parallel to the
railway track, she too
        developed symptoms,
    hysteria, depression,
    a deviant sexualized
    mesmerism. She told us,
not without resistance,
        that she had had an
    education. Her mother
spoke the apt languages.
She said nothing but lacquer.

Lacquer on this. The brain
like a jelly, something trapped
        in it. She views it
with her double-eye, its
        glittering mound
of curvatures, lipid-rich
        broth. We call it in the vulgar
gelatin. We will return to this point
later. For the child rears her head
to the sound of community, which
    she hears as tribe, later mafia.
    She appears to comprehend
but does not the sorrow
    of haggling. Whether she might
come to say it, let's not insure.
But it is here it commences.
The thickenings of lymph, the
persistent shyness, the passions.
        It is endless. As symbol, luxury,
she finds, and poverty are the same.
    She listens prodigally. Correlatives
        appear, disappear. She lacquers
them. But poverty, she finds, is,
        in act, in thought, a word, to her,
    not otherwise permitted, real.
Articulacy then was of elbows
    and knees. The spirit never quite
levels between her mother and
    the woman on the blue tarp,
but they touch hands. The mother
communes with nearly every one.
    The child rears her ugly head,
quizzical. Recrudescence
    that's luscious, shutting down
institutes. Speak, she says, speak,
my heart is gelatin. If anything luxe
        is, it is this severe
unthinkable audio. Palatial,
    she says. In futures glorious

and systematic the word ATELIER
   will come to describe this
      pure fragment, this collapse of lines.
Curvatures, she thinks. Conniptions.
   The dusty, colloidal elegance, she
thinks, of air. She views it with her
      double-eye, sculptural aspect.
A powdery substance overlays things,
steady music. It is here she comes to
      comprehend, tender,
later, smell it. We call it in the vulgar
money. Speak, she speaks. The humors
reside not in but a quarter of an inch
   away from her, settling sometimes
as sweat. She was extraordinarily
   vulnerable, with not even a
rotten core. What might coerce her
   to nostalgia. Hot tea chilled jelly
dissolves. No quality here. It is
      nothing and the saw. The recrude-
scence is luscious, shuts down law.
   It began as tendency. Petty crime.
      Delirium of touching. Passion of
the silk. Subjective correlatives.
   Desire, dark wishes, ossifications,
   and abbreviations of sound. The
refusal to dance, the turning away
      inside the apostrophe. Meditative
processional. It got heavy. She
   lacquered it. She viewed it with her
      vulgar eye. She lacquered it.
         No delicacy obtained. She put it
   away in its pure future, glittering
mound. The opposite of hot tea
   and a biscuit. Lacquer on it.
Endless, mostly. Difficult to discern.
   The conniptions. Cognitions. This kind
of traffick is difficult to curb. But no,
      it did not affect her. No one was

spirited away. This was not the meadow
in which she grew. No one haggled,
no one withdrew. It was as a lacquer
on her.

"namak"
"rasna"
"beauty bar
 of film stars"

Billboards

You Have Aged

Dream Cake

Snug Guns

Preening Machine
Comparable to Sunrise

Don't Peel
like an Onion
& Reek

Museum of Shapes

Purity Is <u>There</u>
Read Him & Weep

Blessed Drones

Turn Toward Your Symptoms

Be the Concentric Mind of Trees

Come, Disperse
in Our Coliseum of Loss

Sing! Sing!

रस ਹੜ

Meaning I Have Held You

Silken Child You Appear to Be
Unraveling

Pins & Needles

Etcetera

"I try to rest in the depressions"

Meadow Interregnum

It is the skyward glance that begins.

Begins to look upon the wind chimes up on the tree.

In the tree, medallions. Jade medallions quivering correlatively.

Color flashing into the feet commits a stirring effect upon the loins.

This feels good.

This feels so good ... that the back should rest ...

and the legs one had too long been upon ... and sinking in the dun earth feels good on the ear ... the ear shifting with the head hits the bicuspid grass ... now it is the bicuspid grass that

begins the ear ... meaning downwardly corresponds its deep wet riot the back bites the deep dun earth yer get shook about for the late few pennies but it just feels so dun ... good ... so good to be given ... pause the eye and ear somewhere in tow ... and somewhere the foot ... the foot that came in a pair goes one then the other the ear grovels in the mud the knee twists toward the sky ... are these

the postures? ... the cunt that lies among the reeds ... is this?

Now it is the cunt that begins. Now it is the skyward glance that stunts thy canny lingual dream that instituted the lying under the tree ... and is this the posture? Doubt has this surface to it

like the skin of milk but on the sea ... the sea that the plain eye and the plain ear observe from their heartland seam ... is this possible

from this body? Doubt has this pleasure to it

like the skin of milk but on the sea and now it is the song that is alveolar now it is the womb that wanders now ... a cloud ... now

it shall rain ... are these the divisions? Feel these ribs, are these?
Feeling has this question to it like

the skin of milk the ear falls to the ground and listens ... coral reef,
receive this ... like the male of the species, receive this ...

Hey u! U ova there! Get outta there!

"Yessir. Yessiree, boss."

Epistle to the Efficience

Dark night. Amazing air. I am held back
under the heat lamp. Before the green tea, I
make the positional statement, I render the fat.
There is a thin line beyond the pale.

In the quiet times, I dine frequently,
elsewhere glimmers as sensory overload, more
acid, more acid, please, fold this as I

report on the recession, the long lines
forming onerous, prismatic hedgerows that fatten
on the rib of neighborly divisions, property
perimeters, icy

brinks all the way down to the corner shop,
the honeyed provisos of kind preachers, changed
execs, sweet peach sellers, long textured
lines, heavy, inalienably

aromatic, as newsprint, as so much
writtenness, it is getting out of hand, my own hands
simply fold.

It gets darker, though it be a metaphor
that is darkness,

and it gets still, though it be a molecular
deception,

and it gets ever more fragrant, though it be
ineffable, and

the sequencing gets shook up,
the conclusion wishes to assert itself but is
concealed,

and so I under the starry metaphor, I inside
the pregnant description, I amid the tenable scents,
I feel simply feelings. Under the arbor,

I sniff the arbore-
scent, I enter its porous wisdom, the crackling in
cinema equal to kindling, for

in some sense
I am reporting on a country, peeking over the fence,
shrieking, look! look! an interiority! look, such a

       private, green
articulation! what a potted frond of despair, this
man speaking his silent monologue, face screwed up
for expression. A camera studies him, lingers on him,
lingers on his objects, whence refracts the whole
of his psychosoma. The room reverberates with this
'curation' of being.
       In the film of this man's life,
which is cavernous, all angularities commiserate.
His ennui is stirring, his rage renascent.
Method and méprise are his calling cards.
       The camera is deft, so I am dire.
I look into the mounting of desire,
       into the diminutive, the moon-dependent
feeling, o that he has a feeling, o that it opens out,
opening out an old sense, system-
atically uncoiling along the soundtrack,
       the appropriate record
from the appropriate decade of his youth,
which shaped his interior, as though from this,
surely, the darkness, metonymic, shall
proceed.
       I fold this.
       I fold all the cinema
I ever grazed upon, bovine, five thousand daisies
pushing senses out of my skin, for although they
showed me the thin line between being and not,
my steady hand and unsteady heart, quote unquote,
       when it is my turn to look 'inside,'
every hesitation that might hesitates me. I write,
'Solace is tainted, nonplussed.' I write, 'No
precision that isn't imprecision.' I observe
       the housekeeper
is an erotomaniac; pixel density and contrast ratio;
multiple refrains and a sort of pulling against
       the consensual seduction; thin lines
meaning hesitation is a certain theory, 'certainty
like a quality of gems and cautious doctrines.' Every
       theory lingers in the cavities

as I lapse from it, prosodies are faithless but
divine. In some sense then, according to a source,
the reports have gone awry. The prolix lines,
the keen sight. And the night is savage, somni-
feral. I remind my oriental mind.

Tomorrow morning, I recover,
take dictation from a swallow or whatever passes
for it. What does it observe? Saline waters,
lines drawn in mud. What do I? I sort
        the idiolects.
'Everything can be studied,' I posit. 'O be obsessed,'
they counter. 'O I will.'
        Then a microphone falls into the trenches.
        Then animals gaze into the eyes of other animals.
        I try to see people for
what they are. An infant. A man. His facial symmetry,
his thinness, his liquid crystal leucoderm, the papery
fullness of his psychology. Thin line going somewhere,
one day perforating ...
        I am a little terrified now.
        I look up toward the sky.
        I see these lovers on a balcony. They lean
against the hard facts. It is argument that tilts them.
        I look up the science in the sky.
What do I see? I see lovers on a balcony, bent over,
isosceles. Then what do I see? The gladiolus?
The eglantine? Prissy mouth shapes? A postcard
with a Klee on it. I fold it. I feel the crease. It is ugly
and imprecise. I feel the wrongness, I forget absence,
forget presence, in the light of day: séjour, cæsura.

It is said, 'A kind of malignant mind
creeps through the earth lit only by the light
of the movies.'
        In the recession, an easterly mind
is unable to give up its ideas, accordion
sea. In a forest of pines, sap pools,
reports go awry, fold this.
        I am reporting on a country.
        There appears a corrosion on its hills.
        Birds are winding its landscape,
using it to tell time.
        The report goes awry.
Again.
        I am reporting on a country.
        There appears a buzzing on its sills.
        There appears a digital sort of graininess.
        A thin line appears, dividing estrangement from
habit, lupines from tentacles, 'a spasm, / a psalm.'
        Again.
        I am reporting on a country.
        Traffic is a lovely lingering sound. Shops are
open. I neglect what neglects me. Feel a bit petty.
I drink a wine, I dress a vegetable, quick kimchi,
slow down!
        Again.
        According to a source, I am reporting on
a country. I am learning some skills, I am wielding them
as others do. I am feeling things as I am wont to do.
What do I observe? Bald classicism. Fallen
romanticism. The stained glass of basement revivals.
What do I learn? Nothing sensible.

'Will you,' she says, 'try not falling
in any Ballardian pools?'

Dark night. Dark theatre. A love
of subtitle files fills me. Narration, speech, voice.
Timestamps secrete a music. When I watch a film
I explore a time 'that is not mine,' 'that is mine,
it is so near to the heart.' The film is a fold. The fold
lies at one end of a woman's body. It lies
murdered in a field. In the gorgeous rolling
country I love the merest christ figures. I love
the thin blades of thin grass, the scurrilous winters,
doxy doxa, o be still, my senseless intel,
            be still, o night
that is metallic, o meticulous human
in the window next door. I've been watching your
interior grow. Roseate
in the roseate light. Not like the rose's shabby
inscape and not like the ball gowns wrinkling
from memory, sartorial
paysan, you are dressed most simply, ruddy
and complex only ever inside. I fold you.
Against my bed you make an impressionism
like a fossil.
            In the recession, away from all
edifications, nasturtiums,
            I am stopped from the couplet
or at the border of a country.
            As ways and truths go,
I am more or less deadened.
            My effete mind rests upon
an effete divan.
            A crocus occurs a.

Darkest of nights. Smell of cyanide.
Cruel jokes circulate. Here are some definitions
of sex, here some anatomies of money.
An impecunious fluid routs my flesh.
　　　'Everyone,' she says, 'everyone
is doing the work but what does the work
do?' I observe the cheap light turn slowly
gibbous, why not. 'The terror,' she says, 'isn't,'
she says, 'we're fragments.' 'The terror is,'
she says, 'we're whole.' The copse witnessed
through the opera glass turns into a
guess what. Fold it.
　　　Dank morning. 'I cultivate a primrose'
that is cryptic. An impresario, I unfold its petals.
　　　Method, méprise. Nostalgia for a condition
gone by, when 'Silk was a duration' and 'I
unpacked it.' A rich, quotidian engagement,
whatever that is, too much of it, too much presence,
too much absence, fold it. Thin line
　　　between vellum and blunt instrument.
Fold it.
　　　Late afternoon. Aspic quivers.
Birds shed their descriptors.
　　　Hopkinsesque accents
equip the air with plain joy, then torqued
pleasure. The imagined cottage, the oblique
approach to which is a romance, sits pretty.
　　　Why a quivering aspic?
　　　This slightly outlandish window into my
—no interior, we said—sensations, the way the
alleged storm affects the globe on a dish upon a
table in the somewhat inclement outside turning
to hell, it shivers
totally.
　　　A quaint time of day even the streets glisten
a dark sort of description. It's all right, don't come.
I'll just 'decay with imprecision.'
　　　The experiment in stillness isn't death, it's
an attempt toward season.

'These prosodies,' she says, 'of hesitation,' she says, 'are spasms,' she says, 'of inquiry.' The analysis wings about the room, aquiline. In some sense,
I have been reporting on a country.
'An alien,' she says. The strain marks a hesitation that grows more resonant as we go on. According to a source, the source will never appear. 'What have you learnt?' she asks.

On a square on her wall a meadow of cows lisps.

'Violence,' she says, 'is not the answer,' perforce.

Wind dissipates mind seeds.
Things I have said return odd.
The future, I said, ought to be the new 'time
lost.'
The sentence, I said, is torqued, I said, at times
to defamiliarize, at times to attain sublime doubt.
The experience is so wild any path you cut through it
cuts through you, so said I
once, on a carousel.

In the recession, it is white.
Alchemically slack, the fruit on my toast.
Dark, gelatinous. Unusual, bejeweled.
Beveled?
My head?
Thin line.

'There is,' I say, 'inside you
an absence.' 'There is,' I say, 'inside you
a presence.' I watch your interior grow.

'Social Gesture' quotes Szilárd Borbély, tr. Ottilie Mulzet ('this strange / affinity'); Bruno Dumont ('sensation / not sense'); Geoffrey Hill ('first then'); and Edmond Jabès, tr. Rosmarie Waldrop ('the sea indents the universe').

'Concerning Matters Culinary' is a spectral Easter egg.

'Emporium' quotes J. H. Prynne ('qualities / as they continue are the silk under the hand').

'"nation"' quotes Percy Bysshe Shelley ('the sense / faints').

'"rhapsody"' quotes Geoffrey Hill ('red') and translates a portion of Ælfric's *Grammar and Glossary*.

'Notes on the Passions of Patient M.' adapts Gaëtan Gatian de Clérambault's *Passion érotique des étoffes chez la femme*.

'Experiment with Aspic' & its epitaph quote and translate Platina ('quod vulgo gelatinam vocamus' + 'we call it in the vulgar gelatin').

'Epistle to the Efficience' quotes Ray Ragosta ('A kind of malignant mind / creeps through the earth lit only by the light / of the movies'); Geoffrey Hill ('a spasm / a psalm'); Robert Duncan ('that is not mine' & 'that is mine, it is / so near to the heart'); *The Hindu* Crossword 11779 by Aspartame ('I cultivate a primrose'); and T. S. Eliot ('decay with imprecision').

MILLES MERCIS

To Marty Cain & Kina Viola for *Prologue* | *Emporium* (Garden-Door Press), and Brian Teare for *Rhapsody* (Albion Books); the editors of *Apartment Poetry, Berkeley Poetry Review, Boston Review, Lana Turner, Poem-a-Day* at poets.org, *Seedings, The Rumpus, The Spectacle,* & *Western Humanities Review* for publishing many of these poems, sometimes in different versions; Mónica de la Torre for the Mountain West Writers' Prize in Poetry 2017; Gillian Conoley, Fady Joudah, & Cole Swensen for recognizing *Emporium* with the James Laughlin Award; the English Departments at University of Denver and Washington University in Saint Louis for institutional support; the Evan Frankel Foundation for a dissertation fellowship; Carla Gullichsen and the Varda Artists Residency Program for three weeks on the extraordinary SS Vallejo where I was able to complete this manuscript; Kazim Ali, Lindsey Boldt, Tiffany Malakooti, Stephen Motika, & all at Nightboat for *this*; Donna Beth Ellard for Old English, Latin, and so much more; Graham Foust for musical thinking, mentorship, and reading these poems a hundred times; Mary Jo Bang, Rachel Feder, Laird Hunt, Jennifer Kronovet, Nithin Manayath, Jennifer Pap, Carl Phillips, Bin Ramke, Selah Saterstrom, Eleni Sikelianos for your teachings and guidance; Kanika Agrawal, Zack Anderson, Mildred Barya, Teresa Carmody, Carolina Ebeid, David Hernandez, Brandi Homan, Poupeh Missaghi, Jeffrey Pethybridge, Allan Popa, Niel Rosenthalis, Michael Joseph Walsh, and S. Yarberry for friendship, kindness, and sustenance; Kelly Caldwell for her unforgettable beauty; Julie Carr, Don Mee Choi, Johannes Göransson, Geoffrey G. O'Brien, Ted Mathys, Joyelle McSweeney, & Divya Victor for gifts that cannot be named; Patty of the thousand names and faces; my family, especially Sid & Suman, and my parents François & Min, I am utterly grateful.

NIGHTBOAT BOOKS

Nightboat Books, a nonprofit organization, seeks to develop audiences for writers whose work resists convention and transcends boundaries. We publish books rich with poignancy, intelligence, and risk. Please visit nightboat.org to learn about our titles and how you can support our future publications.

The following individuals have supported the publication of this book. We thank them for their generosity and commitment to the mission of Nightboat Books:

Kazim Ali
Anonymous
Jean C. Ballantyne
Photios Giovanis
Amanda Greenberger
Elizabeth Motika
Benjamin Taylor
Peter Waldor
Jerrie Whitfield & Richard Motika

In addition, this book has been made possible, in part, by grants from the New York City Department of Cultural Affairs in partnership with the City Council and the New York State Council on the Arts Literature Program.